The limerick form is complex
Its contents run chiefly to sex.
It burgeons with virgeons
And masculine urgeons
And swarms with erotic effects.

In other words
—simply filth!

Also by Roger Kilroy and illustrated by McLachlan

GRAFFITI: THE SCRAWL OF THE WILD
GRAFFITI 2: THE WALLS OF THE WORLD
GRAFFITI 3: THE GOLDEN GRAFFITI AWARDS

and published by Corgi Books

ILLUMINATED LIMERICKS

Compiled and introduced
by Roger Kilroy
Illustrated by McLACHLAN

CORGI BOOKS

A DIVISION OF TRANSWORLD PUBLISHERS LTD

ILLUMINATED LIMERICKS
A CORGI BOOK 0 552 11913 X

First publication in Great Britain

PRINTING HISTORY
Corgi edition published 1982

Copyright © 1982 by Roger Kilroy
Illustrations copyright © 1982 by Edward McLachlan

This book is set in 11 pt. Times Roman

Corgi Books are published by Transworld Publishers Ltd.,
Century House, 61–63 Uxbridge Road,
Ealing, London, W5 5SA

Made and printed in Great Britain by
The Guernsey Press Co. Ltd., Guernsey, Channel Islands.

CONTENTS

INTRODUCTION

According to the dictionary, 'the five-line nonsense verse known as the Limerick originated with the eighteenth century ale-house chorus *Will you come up to Limerick?'*

Rubbish! McLachlan and I have been doing some serious research on the subject and we've unearthed loads of limericks that were doing the rounds way before the beginning of the eighteenth century. This one, for example, is more than five hundred years old:

> Ewe bleateth after lamb,
> Low'th after calve too.
> Bullock starteth
> Bucke farteth—
> Merry sing Cuckoo!

And look at this—without doubt the first limerick in the history of the world:

> In the Garden of Eden lay Adam
> Complacently stroking his madam,
> And loud was his mirth
> For on all of the earth
> There were only two balls—and he had 'em.

Of course that best-known limerick writer was that eminent Victorian Edward Lear (1812–1888):

> Although at the limericks of Lear
> We may be tempted to sneer
> We should never forget
> That we owe him a debt
> For his work as the first pioneer.

The trouble with Lear's limericks is that they do tend to be remarkably respectable . . .

> There was an old person from Twickenham
> Who whipped his four horses to quicken 'em;
> When they stood on one leg
> He said faintly 'I beg
> We may go back directly to Twickenham!'

. . . and the trouble with respectable limericks is that they do tend to be somewhat short on laughs . . .

> The Limerick packs laughs anatomical
> Into space that's quite economical.
> But the good ones I've seen
> So seldom are clean
> And the clean ones so seldom are comical.

Don't misunderstand us. We're honest, clean-living souls, like you. We don't want limericks that are coarse or crude. We are very well aware that a limerick has to be handled with care . . .

> The limerick is furtive and mean;
> You must keep it in close quarantine,
> Or it sneaks to the slums
> And promptly becomes
> Disorderly, drunk and obscene.

As far as we're concerned, in poetry—as in fancy dress —subtlety is all:

> There was a young woman from Aenos
> Who went to a party as Venus.
> We told her how rude
> 'Twas to go there quite nude,
> So we got her a leaf from the green-h'us.

In the course of our rigorous researches McLachlan and I have come across limericks of every description—from limericks that celebrate the great intellectual giants of the age like this one:

> There's a notable family named Stein:
> There's Gertrude, there's Ep and there's Ein.
> Gert's prose is the bunk
> Ep's sculpture is junk
> And no one can understand Ein!

—to limericks that don't look like limericks at all, like the advertisement once placed in the *Catholic Herald* by Monsignor Ronald Knox: 'Evangelical vicar in want of a portable secondhand font, would dispose of the same for a portrait (in frame) of the Bishop Elect of Vermont.'

But the limericks I have chosen and McLachlan has illuminated for this collection are the ones we feel suit the form best. We're both philosophers at heart, so in the pages that follow we've tried to create a unique A to Z of Life with Limericks. We're great believers in *joie de vivre** and by the time you've been through our book we hope you will be too.

R.K.

*That's French for 'grin and bear it'.

ANIMAL MAGIC.

An eccentric old person of Slough,
Who took all his meals with a cow,
Always said, 'It's uncanny,
She's so like Aunt Fanny,'
But he never would indicate how.

The village was giddy with rumours
Of a goat who was suffering from tumors,
Garbage, rubbish and waste
Were all to his taste—
But he choked on Elizabeth's bloomers.

There was an old lady of Herm,
Who tied bows on the tail of a worm;
Said she, 'You look festive,
But don't become restive,
You'll wriggle 'em off if you squirm.'

There was a young girl known as Sue
Who carried a frog in each shoe.
When asked to stop
She replied with a hop
'I'm trying to get in Who's Zoo!'

There was a young girl name of Clare
Who once was attacked by a bear.
While chased in a field
She tripped and revealed
Some meat to the bear that was rare.

Said a cat as he playfully threw
His wife down a well in Peru,
'Relax, dearest Thora,
Please don't be angora,
I was only artesian you.'

There was a young peasant named Gorse
Who fell madly in love with his horse.
Said his wife: 'You rapscallion
That horse is a stallion—
This constitutes grounds for divorce.'

There was a young maid from Madras
Who had a magnificent ass.
Not rounded and pink
As you probably think—
It was grey, had long ears, and ate grass.

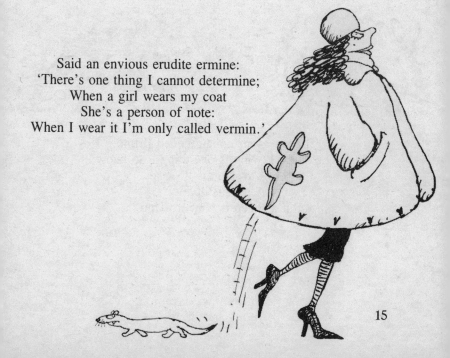

Said an envious erudite ermine:
'There's one thing I cannot determine;
When a girl wears my coat
She's a person of note:
When I wear it I'm only called vermin.'

15

There once was a gnu in a zoo
Who tired of the same daily view.
To seek a new sight
He stole out one night,
And where he went gnobody gnu.

There was an Italian named Bruno
Who said: 'Loving is one thing I do know.
A woman is fine,
A man is divine,
But a sheep is Numero Uno.'

BAD MANNERS.

I sat next to the Duchess at tea.
It was just as I feared it would be:
Her rumblings abdominal
Were simply phenominal,
And everyone thought it was me!

There once was a fellow called Sydney,
Who ate lots of pie—steak and kidney.
He ate so much crust
That they thought he would bust,
He ought to have known better—now didney?

It's the latest on-going thing I believe.

There was a young woman named Dotty
Who said as she sat on her potty,
'It isn't polite
To do this in sight,
But then who am I to be snotty?'

There was a young person from Tottenham
Whose manners, Good Lord! she'd forgotten 'em.
When she went to the Vicar's,
She took off her knickers,
Because she said she was hot in 'em.

We thought him an absolute lamb,
But when he sat down in some jam
On taking his seat
At our Sunday School treat,
We all heard the Vicar say: 'Damn!'

I don't mind if a girl rides a hel'copter,
I don't mind if a girl drives a car,
But the girl who rides straddle
An old fashioned saddle
Is stretching things just a bit far.

There was a young curate of Minster
Who admonished a giddy young spinster.
For she used, on the ice,
Words not at all nice
When he, at a turn, slid against her.

CAMP FOLLOWERS.

There was a young man named Treet
Who minced as he walked down the street.
He wore shoes of bright red,
And playfully said,
'I may not be strong, but I'm sweet.'

A pansy who lived in Khartoum
Took a lesbian up to his room.
They argued all night
Over who had the right
To do what, and with which, and to whom.

There was a gay writer named Smith,
Whose virtue was largely a myth.
We knew that he did it;
He couldn't have hid it—
The question was only who with.

DRESS SENSE.

A model called Suzy Dunbar
Committed a dreadful *faux pas;*
She loosened a stay
In her new *décolleté*
Exposing her *je ne sais quoi!*

There was a young lady of Wilts,
Who walked to the Highlands on stilts.
When they said, 'Oh, how shocking,
To show so much stocking.'
She answered, 'Well, what about kilts?'

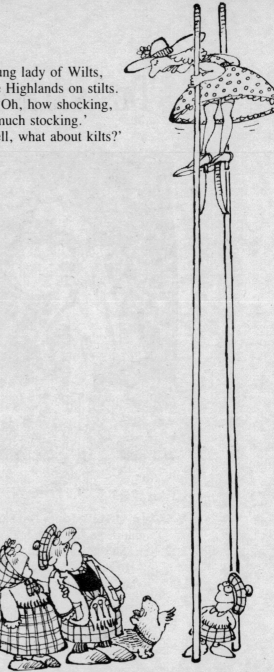

There was a fat lady of Clyde
Whose shoelaces once came untied;
She feared that to bend
Would display her rear end,
So she cried and she cried and she cried.

There once was a girl, Mabel Erskine,
Who had a remarkably fair skin.
When I said to her, 'Mabel,
You'd look well in sable.'
She answered, 'I'm best in my bearskin.'

There was a young lad of Penrose
Who had pockets in none of his clothes.
When asked by his lass
Where he carried his brass
He said: 'Darling, I pay through the nose.'

There once was a lady called Harris
That nothing seemed apt to embarrass
Till the bubble-bath she poured
Into the tub she adored
Turned out to be plaster of Paris.

EGOCENTRIC.

A self-centred old man called Keith
Sat down on his set of false teeth.
Said he, with a start,
'Oh Lor' bless my heart!
I have bitten myself underneath!'

I'd rather have fingers than toes;
I'd rather have ears than a nose;
And as for my hair,
I'm glad that it's there.
I'll be awfully sad when it goes.

An erotic neurotic named Sid
Got his Ego confused with his Id,
His errant libido
Was like a torpedo,
And that's why he done what he did.

A young schizophrenic named Struther
When told of the death of his mother,
    Said, 'Yes, it's too bad,
    But I can't feel too sad.
After all, I *still* have each other.'

The girls who frequent pleasure palaces
Have no use for psychoanalysis.
    And though Doctor Freud
    Would be sorely annoyed,
They stick to their old-fashioned fallacies.

FACTS OF LIFE.

Concerning the birds, bees and flowers
In the gardens, the fields and the bowers,
You will note at a glance
That their ways of romance
Are totally different from ours.

There was an old lady of Harrow
Whose views were exceedingly narrow.
At the end of her paths
She built two bird baths
For the different sexes of sparrow.

There was a young woman from Mulberry,
Whose knowledge of life was desultory,
She announced, like a sage,
'Adolescence is the stage
That comes between puberty and adultery.'

GOLDEN OLDIES.

There was a young man of Devizes,
Whose ears were of different sizes.
The one that was small
Was of no use at all,
But the other won several prizes.

There was a faith-healer of Deal
Who said: 'Although pain isn't real,
  If I sit on a pin,
  And I punctures my skin,
I dislike what I fancy I feel.'

There was a young man of Bengal
Who went to a fancy-dress ball,
  He went, just for fun,
  Dressed up as a bun,
And a dog ate him up in the hall.

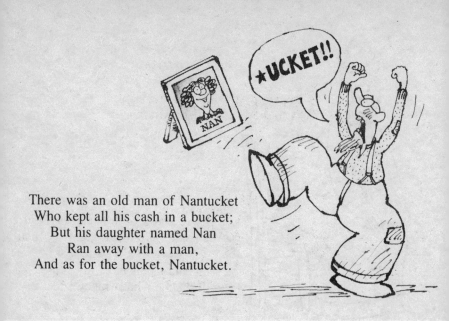

There was an old man of Nantucket
Who kept all his cash in a bucket;
But his daughter named Nan
Ran away with a man,
And as for the bucket, Nantucket.

Said a foolish householder from Wales,
'A foul odour of gas prevails,'
She then struck a light—
And later that night
Was collected in seventeen pails.

HOLIDAY SNAPS.

There was a young lady of Joppa
Who on holiday came quite a 'cropper;
She went to Ostend
With a gentleman friend—
But the rest of the tale is improper.

A signora who strolled down the Corso
Displayed quite a lot of her torso
A crowd soon collected
And no one objected,
Though some were in favour of more so.

A nudist resort at Benares
Took a midget in all unawares,
But he made members weep
For he just couldn't keep
His nose out of private affairs.

Insulting Behaviour.

A girl who weighed many oz.
Used language I dare not pronoz.
For a fellow unkind
Pulled her chair out behind
Just to see (so he said) if she'd boz.

To an artist a husband named Thicket
Said: 'Turn your backside and I'll kick it.
You have painted my wife
In the nude to the life;
Do you think for one moment that's cricket?'

Said a vulgar old Earl, whom I knew:
'I've been struck from the rolls of Who's Who,
Just because I was found,
Lying prone on the ground
With the housemaid; and very nice too!'

There once was a maître d'hôtel
Who said, 'They can all go to hell!
They make love to my wife
And it ruins my life,
For the worst is, they do it so well!'

There was a strange creature named Marks
Whose idea of diversions and larks
Was stirring up tramps,
Disturbing scout log camps,
And defacing nude statues in parks.

A lady there was from Antigua,
Who remarked to her spouse 'What a pigua!'
He retorted 'My Queen,
Is it manners you mean?
Or do you refer to my figua?'

There was a young lady of Bude
Who walked down the street in the nude.
A policeman said, 'Whattum
Magnificent bottom!'
And slapped it as hard as he could.

JUST A DROP.

There was a young fellow called Sydney,
Who drank till he ruined his kidney.
It shrivelled and shrank,
As he sat there and drank,
But he'd had a good time at it, didn' he?

The classic sculptor called Phidias
When drunk was truly invidious.
He carved Aphrodite
Without any nightie,
Which shocked all the purely fastidious.

There was a young lady who tried
A diet of apples, and died.
The unfortunate miss
Really perished of this:
Too much cider inside her inside.

There was a young girl whose frigidity
Approached cataleptic rigidity
Till you gave her a drink
When she quickly would sink
In a state of complaisant liquidity.

There was a young lady named Lynn
Who thought fornication a sin.
But when she was tight
It seemed quite all right—
So the fellows all filled her with gin.

14 men per
gallon, dear

GIN

14 MPG

KEEP FIT.

A lady, an expert on skis,
Went out with a man who said, 'Plis,
On the next precipice
Will you give me a kice?'
She said, 'Quick! Before somebody sis!'

When the tennis ball soared high above,
Nellie rose to receive it like a dove,
But the strain of her reach
Caused her knickers to breach
And her partner to cry out, 'That's love!'

There was a young lady of Venice,
Who used hard-boiled eggs to play tennis.
When they said, 'It seems wrong.'
She remarked, 'Go along!
You don't *know* how prolific my hen is!'

A young girl who was hopeless at tennis
And at swimming was really a menace
Took pains to explain:
'It depends how you train;
I was once a street-walker in Venice.'

There was a young maiden of Siam
Who said to her love, young Kiam,
'If you kiss me, of course
You will have to use force—
But God knows you are stronger than I am.'

LITERARY LAPSES.

There was a young poet of Trinity
Who, although he could trill like a linnet, he
    Could never complete
    Any poem with feet,
Saying, 'Idiots,
    Can't you see
        that what I'm writing
        happens
        to be
        Free
Verse?'

'For the tenth time, dull Daphnis,' said Chloe
'You have told me my bosom is snowy;
    You have made such verse on
    Each part of my person
Now *do* something, there's a good boy!'

Each time she sat down to complete her
    Ode to the famous love cheater,
        The things that he said
        To get her to bed
Seemed to jump off the pages to metre.

If muses be the food of love......

There was a young poet of Thusis
Who took twilight walks with the Muses,
But these nymphs of the air
Are not quite what they were,
And the practice has led to abuses.

49

An authoress armed with a skewer
Once hunted a hostile reviewer.
'I'll teach you,' she cried,
As she punctured his hide,
'To call my last novel too pure!'

The late poet called Ogden Nash
Always made of his English a hash.
When asked where it led
He flippantly said,
'It gives it a great touch of clash.'

There's a clever old miser who tries
Every method to e-con-omize.
He said with a wink,
'I save gallons of ink
By simply not dotting my i's.'

MUSICAL INTERLEWD.

There was an old bass of Boolong
Who frightened the birds with his song.
It wasn't the words
Which astonished the birds
But the horrible *dooble ontong*.

A young violinist from Rio
Was seducing a lady named Cleo.
As she took down her panties
She said, 'No andantes—
I want this *allegro con brio!'*

As Mozart composed a sonata
The maid bent to fasten her garter
Without delay
He started to play
Un poco piu appasionata.

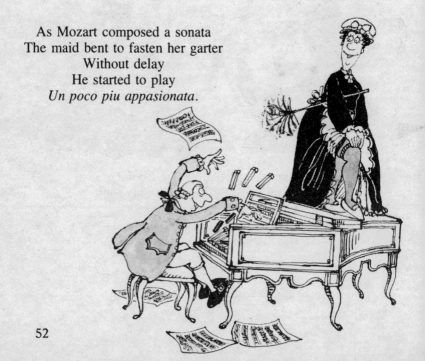

NUPTIAL BLISS.

The bride went up the aisle
In traditional virginal style,
But they say she was nary
An innocent cherry,
But a whore from the banks of the Nile.

A plumpish young lady from Eton
Whose delight was to read Mrs. Beeton
Said: 'Marry me, Jack,
And you'll find that my back
Is a nice place to warm your cold feet on.'

There once was a woman of Churston
Who thought her third husband the worst 'un,
For he justly was reckoned
Far worse than the second,
And her second was worse than the first 'un.

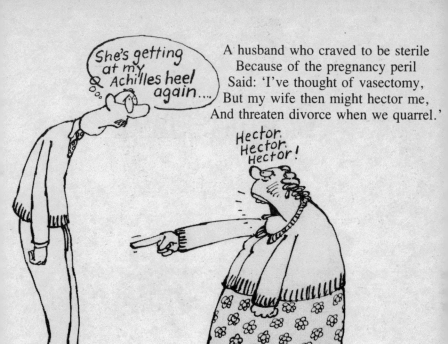

A husband who craved to be sterile
Because of the pregnancy peril
Said: 'I've thought of vasectomy,
But my wife then might hector me,
And threaten divorce when we quarrel.'

There was an old widower, Doyle,
Who wrapped up his wife in tin foil.
He thought it would please her
To stay in the freezer—
And, anyway, outside she'd spoil.

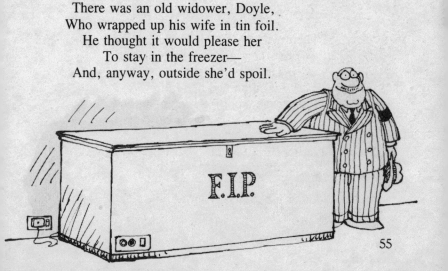

On with the Dance.

There was a young lady named Hall
Wore a newspaper dress to a ball.
The dress caught on fire
And burned her entire
Front page, sporting section and all.

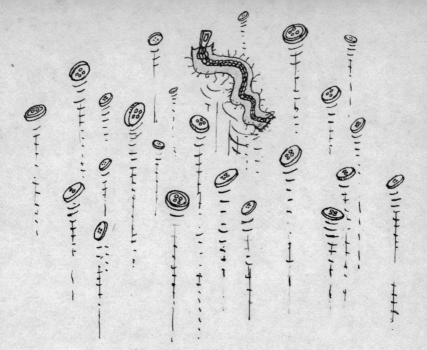

There was a young girl of Darjeeling
Who could dance with exquisite feeling
Not a murmur was heard,
Not a sound, not a word,
But the fly-buttons hitting the ceiling.

A strip-teaser on the Thames River
Caused a sensitive fellow to quiver.
The aesthetic vibration
Brought soulful elation.
Besides, it was good for his liver.

Three young girls from the Bahamas
Attended dance halls in pyjamas.
They were fondled all summer
By sax, bass, and drummer—
I'm surprised that they're not all now mamas.

A nudist by name Horace Sweet
Loved to dance in snow and in sleet,
But one chilly December
He froze every member,
And retired to a monkish retreat.

PREGNANT PAUSES.

There was a young woman from Wantage
Of whom the Town Clerk took advantage.
Said the County Surveyor,
'Of course you must pay her;
You've altered the line of her frontage.'

There was a young lady from Thrace
Whose corsets no longer would lace.
Her mother said, 'Nelly,
There's more in your belly
Than ever went in through your face.'

There was a young lady of York
Who was shortly expecting the stork,
When the doctor walked in
With a businesslike grin,
A pick axe, a spade, and a fork.

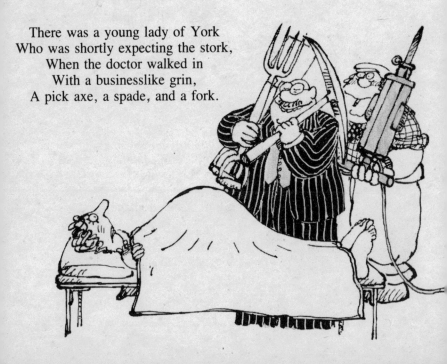

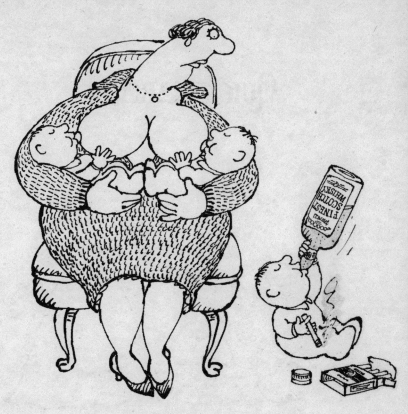

There was a young wife who begat
Three husky boys, Nat, Pat, and Tat.
They all yelled for food,
And a problem ensued
When she found there was no tit for Tat.

When twins came, their father Dann Dunn
Gave 'Edward' as name to each son.
When folks cried 'Absurd!'
He replied 'Ain't you heard
That two Eds are better than one?'

QUICK MARCH!

There was a fierce soldier from Parma,
Who lovingly fondled his charmer.
Said the maiden demure,
'It's delightful, I'm sure,
But it's better without all that armour.'

There was a G.I. from Detroit
Who at kissing was very adroit;
He could pucker his lips
Into total eclipse,
Or open them out like a quoit.

The spouse of a pretty young thing
Came home from the wars in the spring.
He was lame but he came
With his dame like a flame—
A discharge is a wonderful thing.

RELIGIOUS MANIA.

The Dean undressed with heaving breast
The Bishop's wife to lie on.
He thought it lewd
To do it nude
So he kept his old school tie on.

There was a young girl from Odessa,
A somewhat unblushing transgressor.
When sent to the priest
The lewd little beast
Began to undress her confessor.

There once was a monk in Siberia
Whose existence grew steadily drearier,
Till he broke from his cell
With one hell of a yell
And eloped with the Mother Superior.

A prelate of very high station
Was impeached by a pious relation.
He was found in a ditch
With—I won't say a witch—
But a woman of no education.

'oos that, luv?

A potent young monk in a wood
Told a girl she should cling to the good.
She obeyed him—and gladly!
He repulsed her—but sadly;
'My dear, you have misunderstood.'

There was once a Dominican friar
Who was seized with unholy desire;
And the primary cause
Was the Abbess's drawers,
Which were airing in front of the fire.

There once was a monk of Gibraltar
Who wrote dirty jokes in his psalter.
An inhibited nun
Who had read every one
Made a vow to be laid on his altar.

67

Social Intercourse.

There was a young lady of Brent
Who said that she knew what it meant
When he asked her to dine,
Private room, lots of wine,
She knew, oh she knew!—but she went!

There was an old Duchess from Pitlochry
Whose morals were truly a mockery,
For under her bed
Was a lover instead
Of the usual porcelain crockery.

There is a young countess named Maude,
A frightful society fraud.
In company she
Is as cold as can be,
But get her alone—O my Gawd!

There is a young girl of Kilkenny,
Who is worried by lovers so many
That the saucy young elf
Means to raffle herself,
And the tickets are two for a penny

There was a young lady of Leek
Who had fifty proposals a week.
Though she never grew tired
Of being admired,
She was often too sleepy to speak.

A housewife called out with a frown
When surprised by some callers from town,
　　'In a minute or less
　　I'll slip on a dress'—
But she slipped on the stairs and came down.

There was an old fellow from Croydon,
Whose cook was a neat little hoyden.
　　She would sit on his knees
　　While shelling the peas
Or pleasanter duties employed on.

TRAVELLERS' TALES.

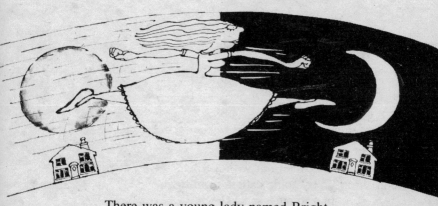

There was a young lady named Bright
Whose speed was far faster than light
She went out one day
In a relative way,
And returned the previous night.

VI–VA ESPANA

There was a young lady of Spain
Who took down her pants on the train.
There was a young porter
Saw more than he orter,
And asked her to do it again.

A beautiful creature called Jane
Once kissed every man on a train;
Said she, 'Please don't panic;
I'm just nymphomanic—
It wouldn't be fun were I sane.'

There once was a fellow named Vane,
Whose leg was chopped off by a train.
　　When his friend said: 'How sad.'
　　He replied: 'It's not so bad,
For it's cured my varicose vein.'

There was a young fellow from Tyne
Put his head on the South-Eastern Line;
　　But he died of ennui,
　　For the 5.53
Didn't come till a quarter past nine.

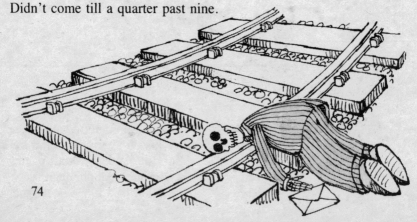

Unloved & Alone.

A homely old spinster of France
Who all men looked at askance,
Threw her skirt overhead
And then jumped into bed,
Saying, 'Now I've at least half a chance.'

A short-sighted spinster named White
Wore a suit of pyjamas one night.
As she happened to pass
In front of a glass
She exclaimed: 'There's a man!' in delight.

There was once an old maid of Worcester
Who dreamt that a rooster seduced her.
She woke with a scream,
But 'twas only a dream—
A bump in the mattress had goosed her.

There was once a girl young and witty,
Who in looks was really quite pretty—
Yet one can't help but know
She has dreadful B.O.
As she's pretty and witty, it's a pity.

There was an old maid name of Rood,
Who was such an absolute prude
That she pulled down the blind
When changing her mind
Lest a libidinous eye should intrude.

VULGAR TONGUES.

There was a young girl of Tralee,
Whose knowledge of French was 'Oui, oui.'
When they said: 'Parlez-vous?'
She replied: 'Same to you!'
And was famed for her bright repartee.

There was a young charmer named Sheba
Whose pet was a darling amoeba.
This queer blob of jelly
Would lie on her belly,
And blissfully murmur, *'Ich liebe.'*

In Paris some visitors go
To see what no person should know
And then there are tourists,
The purest of purists,
Who say it is quite *comme il faut*.

There was a young fellow called Rex
With diminutive organs of sex.
When charged with exposure,
He said with composure:
'De minimus no curat lex!'

There was a young lady named Prentice
Who had an affair with a dentist.
To make the thing easier
He used anaesthesia,
And diddled her *non compos mentis*.

WATER NYMPHS.

A buxom young lady of Bude
Remarked: 'Men are exceedingly rude;
When I bathe in the sea
They all follow me
To see if my bosoms protrude.

There was a young lady named Zanka
Who retired while the ship lay at anchor;
But awoke in dismay
When she heard the mate say:
'We must pull up the top sheet and spanker.'

There was a proud sailor named Bates
Who did the fandango on skates.
He fell on his cutlass
Which rendered him nutless
And practically useless on dates.

Once a bather's clothing was strewd
By winds that left her quite nude.
Soon a man came along—
And unless I am wrong
You expected this line to be lewd.

A fisherman off of Quobod
Said 'I'll catch that tuna, by God!'
But the high-minded fish
Resented his wish
And nimbly swam off with his rod.

X-Censored.

In this book you will have to admit
There are certain rude words we omit.
It would be very bad luck
If you found the word f***
And we never, no never, use s***.

There were three young ladies of Birmingham
And this is the scandal concerning 'em.
As they knelt in their stalls
They tickled the *****
Of the Bishop engaged in confirming 'em.

YOUTHFUL FANCIES.

A much-worried mother once said,
'My dear, you've been kissing young Fred
Since six; it's now ten.
Do it just once again,
And then think of going to bed.'

When her daughter got married in Bicester
Her mother remarked as she kissed her,
'That fellow you've won
Is sure to be fun—
Since tea he's kissed me and your sister.'

There were once two young people of taste
Who were beautiful down to the waist
So they limited love
To the regions above,
And thus remained perfectly chaste.

A young girl who'd not be disgraced
Would flee from all lovers in haste.
It all went quite well
Till one day she fell . . .
She sometimes still dreams that she's chaste.

A cautious young girl from Penzance
Decided to take just one chance.
She wavered, then lo,
She let herself go . . .
Now all of her sisters are aunts.

On Matilda's white bosom there leaned
The cheek of an immature fiend,
But she yanked up his head
And sarcastically said,
'My boy! Won't you *ever* be weaned?'

There was a young maid of Ostend,
Who swore she's hold out to the end;
But alas! half-way over,
Twixt Calais and Dover,
She done what she didn't intend.

Calais-Dover

ZEST FOR LIFE.

A sculptor remarked, 'I'm afraid
I've fallen in love with my trade.
I'm much too elated
With what I've created
And, chiefly, the woman I've made.'

When Angelico worked in cerise,
For the angel he painted his niece.
In a heavenly trance
He pulled off her pants
And erected a fine altar-piece.

While Titian was mixing rose-madder
His model posed nude on a ladder.
Her position, to Titian,
Suggested coition,
So he climbed up the ladder and had 'er.

A greedy young lady named Dee,
Went to bed with each man she did see.
When it came to the test
She wished to be best,
And practice makes perfect, you see.

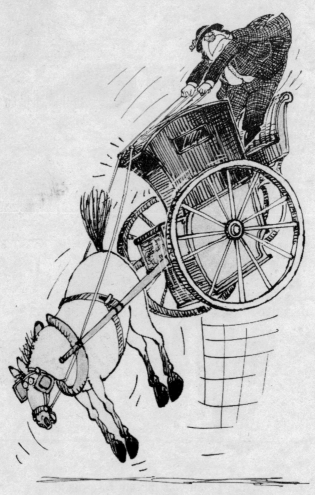

There was a young lady named Ransom
Who was indulged in three times in a hansom.
When she cried out for more
A voice from the floor
Said, 'My name is Simpson, not Samson.'

There was a young lady of Exeter,
So pretty, that men craned their necks at her.
One was even so brave
As to take out and wave
The distinguishing mark of his sex to her.

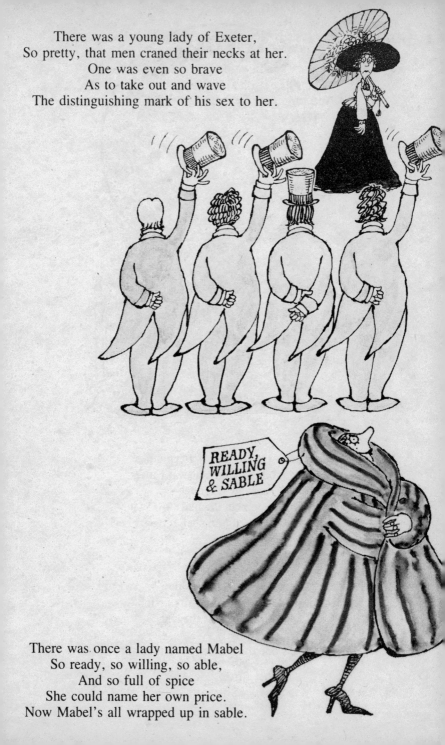

READY,
WILLING
& SABLE

There was once a lady named Mabel
So ready, so willing, so able,
And so full of spice
She could name her own price.
Now Mabel's all wrapped up in sable.

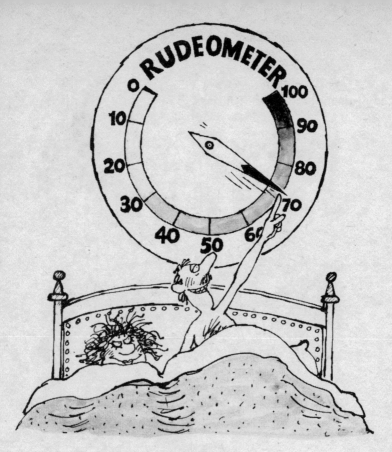

I wooed a stewed nude in Bermuda,
I was rude, but by God! she was ruder.
She said it was crude—
To be wooed in the nude—
I pursued her, subdued her, then screwed her!

'Austerity now is the fashion,'
Remarked a young lady with passion.
Then she glanced at the bed,
And quietly said,
'But there's one thing no one can ration.'

There was a young lady of Norway
Who hung by her heels from a doorway.
She said to her boy
'Just look at me, Roy,
I think I've discovered one more way.'

Said a beautiful girl named Elaine,
'I like it just now and again;
But I wish to explain
That by, 'Now and again'
I mean now and *again* and AGAIN.

God's plan made a hopeful beginning,
But man spoiled his chances by sinning.
We trust that God's Glory
Will end up the story,
But at present the other side's winning!